Mental Maths Every Day for ages 6–7

Dear Parents,

Thank you for buying this copy of *Mental Maths Every Day 6–7*, one of a six book series of maths practice books for primary aged children.

Why is mental maths so important?
All children need to know number facts so that they can remember them instantly when working on more complex aspects of maths. Children who are confident in mental maths also tend to be more confident when faced with money, time, measurements and other mathematical concepts.

This book is designed to boost children's confidence by giving them plenty of practice in quick calculations. The calculations become progressively more difficult as the child works through the book. Don't be surprised if the first few pages seem easy – it's still important that your child completes them. Your child will find some of the other pages very difficult but this is quite normal too; just be on hand to provide help and guidance when needed.

How do I use the book?
Each page of this book is split into columns of questions that have been specially devised for children aged 6–7. Using a stopwatch or clock, ask your child to do as many questions as possible from the first column in exactly one minute. Allow your child to use fingers or counters if she/he needs to. Prompt your child to look very carefully at each question, paying special attention to the mathematical symbol – for example, whether it is an instruction to add or subtract.

At the end of the minute, mark the questions with your child and write down the score for the column in the score box. To save time, the answers are provided on pages 30 to 32. Your child probably won't have time to complete all the questions in the column but praise her/him for trying hard and doing as many as possible. Take the opportunity to discuss any mistakes that have been made and show the child how to do any questions that have been missed out. When she/he is ready your child can complete the next column and try and improve the score. Don't worry if it doesn't improve immediately – 'practice makes perfect' and the improvement in performance will take place sooner or later. Remember that the best way to help is to give lots of praise for success and lots of support where the child is experiencing any difficulty. I do hope that your child enjoys working through the activities.

Andrew Brodie

Contents

Adding numbers up to 10

See if you can answer each set of 12 questions in one minute.

6 + 4 =	1 + 8 =	1 + 7 =
3 + 5 =	4 + 6 =	4 + 2 =
2 + 7 =	5 + 3 =	1 + 6 =
5 + 2 =	2 + 5 =	8 + 2 =
9 + 1 =	7 + 3 =	4 + 5 =
3 + 2 =	5 + 5 =	4 + 4 =
1 + 4 =	1 + 3 =	7 + 2 =
4 + 5 =	5 + 4 =	3 + 4 =
7 + 1 =	6 + 3 =	6 + 1 =
1 + 5 =	2 + 7 =	3 + 3 =
4 + 3 =	5 + 1 =	2 + 4 =
2 + 6 =	3 + 6 =	6 + 2 =

Score

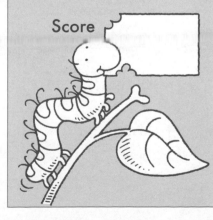

Score

Score

For answers see page 30

See if you can answer each set of 12 questions in one minute.

9 − 3 = ☐
5 − 2 = ☐
8 − 2 = ☐
7 − 1 = ☐
6 − 3 = ☐
4 − 1 = ☐
7 − 3 = ☐
4 − 3 = ☐
6 − 4 = ☐
7 − 2 = ☐
9 − 5 = ☐
5 − 3 = ☐

Score ☐

7 − 6 = ☐
5 − 2 = ☐
8 − 3 = ☐
7 − 4 = ☐
9 − 2 = ☐
6 − 2 = ☐
5 − 4 = ☐
4 − 2 = ☐
8 − 5 = ☐
6 − 1 = ☐
9 − 7 = ☐
3 − 2 = ☐

Score ☐

8 − 7 = ☐
9 − 4 = ☐
5 − 3 = ☐
7 − 5 = ☐
9 − 6 = ☐
8 − 4 = ☐
9 − 5 = ☐
6 − 5 = ☐
7 − 4 = ☐
9 − 8 = ☐
5 − 4 = ☐
8 − 6 = ☐

Score ☐

For answers see page 30

Adding and subtracting up to 10

See if you can answer each set of 12 questions in one minute.

6 + 3 =	5 + 3 =	6 + 2 =
9 − 5 =	8 − 4 =	7 − 4 =
5 + 4 =	6 + 4 =	8 + 1 =
7 − 2 =	5 − 3 =	4 − 2 =
2 + 5 =	2 + 6 =	1 + 7 =
4 − 3 =	9 − 7 =	9 − 6 =
7 + 2 =	1 + 4 =	3 + 2 =
5 − 2 =	6 − 3 =	8 − 5 =
1 + 5 =	4 + 5 =	7 + 1 =
7 − 3 =	7 − 6 =	7 − 5 =
3 + 4 =	2 + 8 =	5 + 5 =
2 − 1 =	5 − 4 =	8 − 7 =

Score

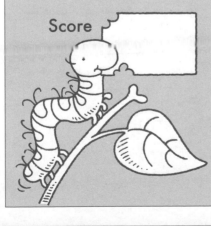

Score

Score

Adding numbers up to 20

See if you can answer each set of 12 questions in one minute.

12 + 5 =	14 + 3 =	11 + 6 =
16 + 3 =	13 + 5 =	12 + 3 =
11 + 4 =	19 + 1 =	14 + 5 =
15 + 2 =	16 + 4 =	18 + 2 =
12 + 4 =	15 + 5 =	11 + 3 =
10 + 6 =	11 + 7 =	15 + 4 =
14 + 4 =	17 + 2 =	11 + 8 =
11 + 5 =	11 + 1 =	13 + 7 =
13 + 3 =	12 + 6 =	13 + 2 =
18 + 1 =	15 + 3 =	10 + 3 =
16 + 2 =	17 + 1 =	14 + 6 =
17 + 3 =	13 + 6 =	12 + 8 =

Score

Score

Score

For answers see page 30

Subtracting numbers up to 20

See if you can answer each set of 12 questions in one minute.

13 − 6 =	16 − 4 =	13 − 5 =
18 − 1 =	17 − 2 =	17 − 1 =
15 − 5 =	19 − 4 =	14 − 6 =
17 − 6 =	11 − 6 =	13 − 8 =
14 − 3 =	15 − 2 =	20 − 7 =
20 − 6 =	17 − 3 =	11 − 5 =
12 − 3 =	19 − 7 =	16 − 9 =
18 − 9 =	12 − 4 =	12 − 5 =
16 − 2 =	11 − 3 =	13 − 9 =
15 − 4 =	14 − 5 =	14 − 7 =
14 − 6 =	13 − 7 =	11 − 4 =
13 − 2 =	12 − 8 =	18 − 5 =

Score

Score

Score

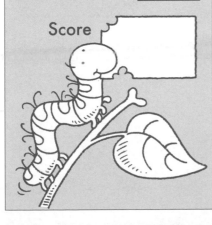

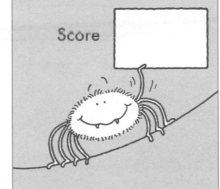

Adding and subtracting up to 20

See if you can answer each set of 12 questions in one minute.

11 + 4 = ☐	16 – 2 = ☐	16 – 9 = ☐
13 – 8 = ☐	11 + 7 = ☐	11 + 3 = ☐
15 + 2 = ☐	13 + 5 = ☐	18 – 9 = ☐
16 – 4 = ☐	15 – 4 = ☐	15 + 4 = ☐
12 + 4 = ☐	11 + 1 = ☐	11 + 8 = ☐
17 – 2 = ☐	14 – 6 = ☐	13 – 2 = ☐
11 + 5 = ☐	13 – 5 = ☐	13 + 7 = ☐
19 – 7 = ☐	17 + 2 = ☐	14 – 5 = ☐
12 – 4 = ☐	20 – 6 = ☐	14 + 6 = ☐
13 + 3 = ☐	12 + 6 = ☐	13 – 7 = ☐
19 – 4 = ☐	12 – 3 = ☐	17 + 1 = ☐
16 + 2 = ☐	15 + 3 = ☐	12 – 8 = ☐

Score ☐

Score ☐

Score ☐

Adding one-digit numbers to two-digit numbers

See if you can answer each set of 12 questions in one minute.

17 + 6 =

28 + 4 =

35 + 6 =

29 + 5 =

48 + 6 =

39 + 8 =

44 + 7 =

58 + 4 =

47 + 6 =

39 + 3 =

63 + 9 =

25 + 8 =

Score

32 + 9 =

18 + 6 =

27 + 6 =

45 + 7 =

12 + 9 =

57 + 5 =

26 + 6 =

57 + 4 =

34 + 8 =

78 + 4 =

55 + 9 =

69 + 5 =

Score

87 + 4 =

54 + 7 =

38 + 6 =

82 + 9 =

17 + 8 =

26 + 7 =

16 + 5 =

28 + 6 =

49 + 9 =

54 + 7 =

29 + 3 =

44 + 8 =

Score

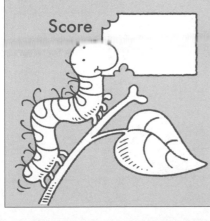

Subtracting one-digit numbers from two-digit numbers

See if you can answer each set of 12 questions in one minute.

62 – 5 =

56 – 7 =

34 – 8 =

78 – 6 =

20 – 5 =

54 – 8 =

35 – 6 =

12 – 4 =

43 – 7 =

27 – 9 =

60 – 4 =

55 – 8 =

Score

22 – 4 =

64 – 5 =

72 – 4 =

80 – 3 =

38 – 5 =

53 – 6 =

84 – 9 =

51 – 5 =

44 – 8 =

71 – 2 =

76 – 9 =

65 – 7 =

Score

40 – 5 =

23 – 4 =

43 – 6 =

21 – 7 =

63 – 4 =

77 – 9 =

34 – 6 =

52 – 5 =

18 – 9 =

42 – 4 =

36 – 7 =

41 – 3 =

Score

For answers see page 30

Adding and subtracting one-digit and two-digit numbers

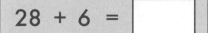

See if you can answer each set of 12 questions in one minute.

28 + 6 =	35 - 6 =	80 - 3 =
78 - 6 =	57 + 5 =	26 + 6 =
34 + 8 =	76 - 9 =	36 - 7 =
20 - 5 =	39 + 8 =	78 + 4 =
39 + 3 =	56 - 7 =	82 + 9 =
12 - 4 =	58 + 4 =	41 - 3 =
62 - 5 =	65 - 7 =	26 + 6 =
63 + 9 =	12 + 9 =	60 - 4 =
27 - 9 =	40 - 5 =	45 + 7 =
26 + 7 =	49 + 9 =	55 - 8 =
54 - 8 =	18 - 9 =	26 + 6 =
47 + 6 =	16 + 5 =	22 - 4 =

Score

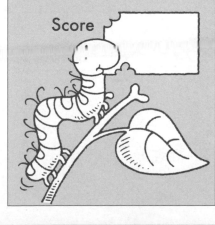

Score

Score

The 2 times table

See if you can answer each set of 12 questions in one minute.

1 × 2 =	4 × 2 =	11 × 2 =
2 × 2 =	11 × 2 =	7 × 2 =
3 × 2 =	8 × 2 =	2 × 2 =
4 × 2 =	5 × 2 =	12 × 2 =
5 × 2 =	9 × 2 =	9 × 2 =
6 × 2 =	2 × 2 =	4 × 2 =
7 × 2 =	6 × 2 =	10 × 2 =
8 × 2 =	10 × 2 =	1 × 2 =
9 × 2 =	7 × 2 =	6 × 2 =
10 × 2 =	12 × 2 =	8 × 2 =
11 × 2 =	1 × 2 =	5 × 2 =
12 × 2 =	3 × 2 =	3 × 2 =

Score

Score

Score

For answers see page 31

Dividing by 2

See if you can answer each set of 12 questions in one minute.

$8 \div 2 =$

$14 \div 2 =$

$2 \div 2 =$

$6 \div 2 =$

$10 \div 2 =$

$18 \div 2 =$

$12 \div 2 =$

$24 \div 2 =$

$4 \div 2 =$

$22 \div 2 =$

$16 \div 2 =$

$20 \div 2 =$

$6 \div 2 =$

$20 \div 2 =$

$8 \div 2 =$

$18 \div 2 =$

$14 \div 2 =$

$2 \div 2 =$

$10 \div 2 =$

$24 \div 2 =$

$16 \div 2 =$

$4 \div 2 =$

$12 \div 2 =$

$22 \div 2 =$

$10 \div 2 =$

$2 \div 2 =$

$18 \div 2 =$

$12 \div 2 =$

$20 \div 2 =$

$24 \div 2 =$

$8 \div 2 =$

$14 \div 2 =$

$22 \div 2 =$

$6 \div 2 =$

$16 \div 2 =$

$4 \div 2 =$

Score

Score

Score

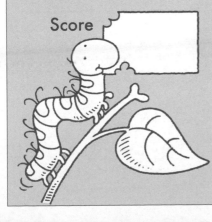

For answers see page 31

13

Multiplying and dividing by 2

See if you can answer each set of 12 questions in one minute.

2 × 2 =	12 × 2 =	12 ÷ 2 =
4 ÷ 2 =	16 ÷ 2 =	8 × 2 =
4 × 2 =	6 ÷ 2 =	10 × 2 =
24 ÷ 2 =	7 × 2 =	18 ÷ 2 =
5 × 2 =	18 ÷ 2 =	6 × 2 =
8 ÷ 2 =	1 × 2 =	4 ÷ 2 =
9 × 2 =	20 ÷ 2 =	12 × 2 =
14 ÷ 2 =	8 × 2 =	20 ÷ 2 =
3 × 2 =	12 ÷ 2 =	7 × 2 =
2 ÷ 2 =	10 × 2 =	16 ÷ 2 =
11 × 2 =	6 × 2 =	11 × 2 =
10 ÷ 2 =	22 ÷ 2 =	14 ÷ 2 =

Score

Score

Score

For answers see page 31

The 5 times table

See if you can answer each set of 12 questions in one minute.

1 x 5 = ☐
2 x 5 = ☐
3 x 5 = ☐
4 x 5 = ☐
5 x 5 = ☐
6 x 5 = ☐
7 x 5 = ☐
8 x 5 = ☐
9 x 5 = ☐
10 x 5 = ☐
11 x 5 = ☐
12 x 5 = ☐

Score ☐

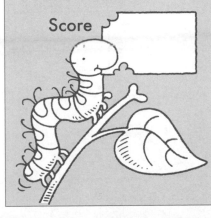

4 x 5 = ☐
2 x 5 = ☐
7 x 5 = ☐
10 x 5 = ☐
5 x 5 = ☐
8 x 5 = ☐
1 x 5 = ☐
12 x 5 = ☐
9 x 5 = ☐
3 x 5 = ☐
6 x 5 = ☐
11 x 5 = ☐

Score ☐

8 x 5 = ☐
2 x 5 = ☐
6 x 5 = ☐
11 x 5 = ☐
3 x 5 = ☐
7 x 5 = ☐
10 x 5 = ☐
4 x 5 = ☐
1 x 5 = ☐
9 x 5 = ☐
5 x 5 = ☐
12 x 5 = ☐

Score ☐

For answers see page 31

Dividing by 5

See if you can answer each set of 12 questions in one minute.

15 ÷ 5 =	25 ÷ 5 =	50 ÷ 5 =
10 ÷ 5 =	10 ÷ 5 =	35 ÷ 5 =
50 ÷ 5 =	30 ÷ 5 =	15 ÷ 5 =
35 ÷ 5 =	60 ÷ 5 =	40 ÷ 5 =
5 ÷ 5 =	15 ÷ 5 =	25 ÷ 5 =
60 ÷ 5 =	45 ÷ 5 =	10 ÷ 5 =
45 ÷ 5 =	50 ÷ 5 =	5 ÷ 5 =
25 ÷ 5 =	35 ÷ 5 =	55 ÷ 5 =
30 ÷ 5 =	5 ÷ 5 =	60 ÷ 5 =
40 ÷ 5 =	20 ÷ 5 =	20 ÷ 5 =
55 ÷ 5 =	55 ÷ 5 =	30 ÷ 5 =
20 ÷ 5 =	40 ÷ 5 =	45 ÷ 5 =

Score

Score

Score

16

For answers see page 31

Multiplying and dividing by 5

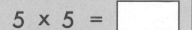

See if you can answer each set of 12 questions in one minute.

5 × 5 =	11 × 5 =	45 ÷ 5 =
12 × 5 =	10 ÷ 5 =	3 × 5 =
50 ÷ 5 =	5 ÷ 5 =	10 × 5 =
8 × 5 =	1 × 5 =	2 × 5 =
35 ÷ 5 =	6 × 5 =	50 ÷ 5 =
2 × 5 =	55 ÷ 5 =	55 ÷ 5 =
15 ÷ 5 =	4 × 5 =	6 × 5 =
6 × 5 =	60 ÷ 5 =	5 × 5 =
40 ÷ 5 =	9 × 5 =	35 ÷ 5 =
10 × 5 =	20 ÷ 5 =	20 ÷ 5 =
25 ÷ 5 =	7 × 5 =	7 × 5 =
11 × 5 =	30 ÷ 5 =	5 ÷ 5 =

Score

Score

Score

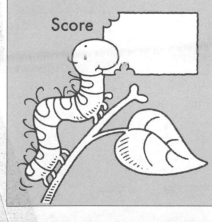

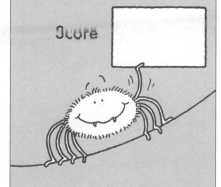

The 10 times table

See if you can answer each set of 12 questions in one minute.

1 × 10 =	7 × 10 =	6 × 10 =
2 × 10 =	4 × 10 =	4 × 10 =
3 × 10 =	2 × 10 =	2 × 10 =
4 × 10 =	12 × 10 =	10 × 10 =
5 × 10 =	6 × 10 =	8 × 10 =
6 × 10 =	10 × 10 =	3 × 10 =
7 × 10 =	1 × 10 =	7 × 10 =
8 × 10 =	9 × 10 =	1 × 10 =
9 × 10 =	3 × 10 =	5 × 10 =
10 × 10 =	11 × 10 =	12 × 10 =
11 × 10 =	5 × 10 =	9 × 10 =
12 × 10 =	8 × 10 =	11 × 10 =

Score

Score

Score

For answers see page 31

Dividing by 10

See if you can answer each set of 12 questions in one minute.

60 ÷ 10 =	50 ÷ 10 =	90 ÷ 10 =
90 ÷ 10 =	20 ÷ 10 =	110 ÷ 10 =
10 ÷ 10 =	80 ÷ 10 =	50 ÷ 10 =
30 ÷ 10 =	100 ÷ 10 =	10 ÷ 10 =
80 ÷ 10 =	60 ÷ 10 =	120 ÷ 10 =
100 ÷ 10 =	120 ÷ 10 =	30 ÷ 10 =
20 ÷ 10 =	70 ÷ 10 =	80 ÷ 10 =
120 ÷ 10 =	110 ÷ 10 =	20 ÷ 10 =
50 ÷ 10 =	10 ÷ 10 =	60 ÷ 10 =
70 ÷ 10 =	30 ÷ 10 =	40 ÷ 10 =
40 ÷ 10 =	90 ÷ 10 =	100 ÷ 10 =
110 ÷ 10 =	20 ÷ 10 =	70 ÷ 10 =

Score

Score

Score

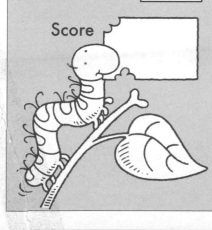

For answers see page 31

Multiplying and dividing by 10

See if you can answer each set of 12 questions in one minute.

70 ÷ 10 = ☐

3 × 10 = ☐

90 ÷ 10 = ☐

110 ÷ 10 = ☐

5 × 10 = ☐

50 ÷ 10 = ☐

7 × 10 = ☐

60 ÷ 10 = ☐

8 × 10 = ☐

50 ÷ 10 = ☐

2 × 10 = ☐

120 ÷ 10 = ☐

Score ☐

5 × 10 = ☐

9 × 10 = ☐

20 ÷ 10 = ☐

4 × 10 = ☐

60 ÷ 10 = ☐

11 × 10 = ☐

50 ÷ 10 = ☐

10 × 10 = ☐

30 ÷ 10 = ☐

8 × 10 = ☐

80 ÷ 10 = ☐

6 × 10 = ☐

Score ☐

120 ÷ 10 = ☐

8 × 10 = ☐

12 × 10 = ☐

70 ÷ 10 = ☐

3 × 10 = ☐

80 ÷ 10 = ☐

5 × 10 = ☐

100 ÷ 10 = ☐

7 × 10 = ☐

60 ÷ 10 = ☐

6 × 10 = ☐

40 ÷ 10 = ☐

Score ☐

For answers see page 31

Doubling numbers up to 10

See if you can answer each set of 12 questions in one minute.

double 6 =

double 8 =

double 5 =

double 3 =

double 1 =

double 9 =

double 7 =

double 10 =

double 2 =

double 4 =

double 3 =

double 7 =

Score

double 8 =

double 2 =

double 9 =

double 6 =

double 4 =

double 1 =

double 8 =

double 3 =

double 5 =

double 7 =

double 10 =

double 6 =

Score

double 8 =

double 9 =

double 1 =

double 2 =

double 7 =

double 4 =

double 10 =

double 3 =

double 8 =

double 5 =

double 2 =

double 6 =

Score

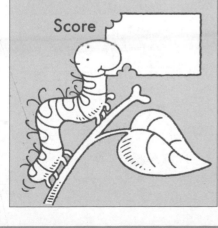
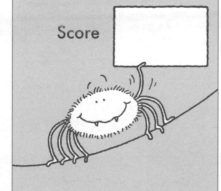

For answers see page 32

Doubling numbers from 11 to 20

See if you can answer each set of 12 questions in one minute.

double 16 =

double 18 =

double 12 =

double 20 =

double 11 =

double 13 =

double 19 =

double 15 =

double 11 =

double 14 =

double 17 =

double 18 =

Score

double 19 =

double 12 =

double 16 =

double 13 =

double 11 =

double 17 =

double 19 =

double 14 =

double 18 =

double 11 =

double 15 =

double 20 =

Score

double 16 =

double 19 =

double 13 =

double 11 =

double 15 =

double 20 =

double 17 =

double 16 =

double 14 =

double 12 =

double 18 =

double 13 =

Score

For answers see page 32

Doubling numbers up to 20

See if you can answer each set of 12 questions in one minute.

double 1 =	double 6 =	double 10 =
double 8 =	double 14 =	double 5 =
double 15 =	double 3 =	double 17 =
double 9 =	double 19 =	double 12 =
double 10 =	double 12 =	double 6 =
double 4 =	double 7 =	double 7 =
double 17 =	double 4 =	double 15 =
double 12 =	double 18 =	double 9 =
double 2 =	double 15 =	double 18 =
double 13 =	double 9 =	double 13 =
double 20 =	double 11 =	double 8 =
double 5 =	double 17 =	double 19 =

Score

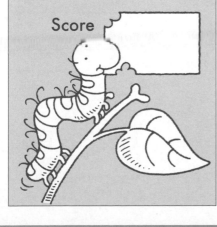

Score

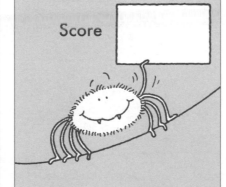

Score

For answers see page 32

Halving even numbers up to 20

See if you can answer each set of 12 questions in one minute.

half of 12 =	
half of 8 =	
half of 16 =	
half of 14 =	
half of 2 =	
half of 20 =	
half of 18 =	
half of 6 =	
half of 10 =	
half of 8 =	
half of 16 =	
half of 4 =	

Score

half of 18 =	
half of 4 =	
half of 12 =	
half of 8 =	
half of 14 =	
half of 10 =	
half of 2 =	
half of 6 =	
half of 14 =	
half of 20 =	
half of 4 =	
half of 16 =	

Score

half of 6 =	
half of 18 =	
half of 12 =	
half of 16 =	
half of 8 =	
half of 14 =	
half of 20 =	
half of 4 =	
half of 12 =	
half of 2 =	
half of 10 =	
half of 18 =	

Score

For answers see page 32

Halving odd numbers up to 20

See if you can answer each set of 12 questions in one minute.

half of 5 =	half of 15 =	half of 5 =
half of 11 =	half of 7 =	half of 13 =
half of 17 =	half of 11 =	half of 19 =
half of 3 =	half of 5 =	half of 1 =
half of 1 =	half of 19 =	half of 15 =
half of 19 =	half of 13 =	half of 17 =
half of 9 =	half of 9 =	half of 7 =
half of 15 =	half of 3 =	half of 11 =
half of 7 =	half of 1 =	half of 19 =
half of 13 =	half of 17 =	half of 3 =
half of 5 =	half of 3 =	half of 9 =
half of 3 =	half of 19 =	half of 15 =

Score

Score

Score

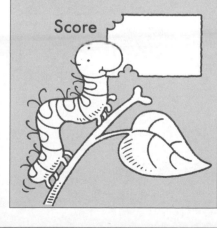

For answers see page 32

Halving numbers up to 20

See if you can answer each set of 12 questions in one minute.

half of 12 =	half of 11 =	half of 5 =
half of 14 =	half of 20 =	half of 13 =
half of 8 =	half of 4 =	half of 16 =
half of 3 =	half of 15 =	half of 2 =
half of 20 =	half of 9 =	half of 19 =
half of 7 =	half of 2 =	half of 6 =
half of 10 =	half of 17 =	half of 14 =
half of 18 =	half of 1 =	half of 18 =
half of 5 =	half of 12 =	half of 4 =
half of 6 =	half of 16 =	half of 17 =
half of 16 =	half of 13 =	half of 9 =
half of 17 =	half of 7 =	half of 15 =

Score

Score

Score

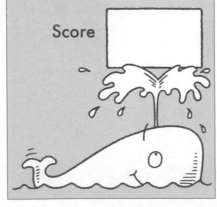

For answers see page 32

Missing numbers in additions up to 20

See if you can answer each set of 12 questions in one minute.

7 +	= 13		6 +	= 12		10 +	= 19
4 +	= 10		9 +	= 17		13 +	= 17
5 +	= 15		3 +	= 10		9 +	= 15
10 +	= 17		7 +	= 16		11 +	= 20
8 +	= 14		15 +	= 18		15 +	= 19
13 +	= 18		5 +	= 16		8 +	= 15
6 +	= 11		14 +	= 17		12 +	= 19
9 +	= 16		8 +	= 10		4 +	= 15
13 +	= 19		11 +	= 19		14 +	= 20
3 +	= 12		16 +	= 20		7 +	= 15
11 +	= 16		5 +	= 17		6 +	= 18
12 +	= 18		12 +	= 15		13 +	= 20

Score

Score

Score

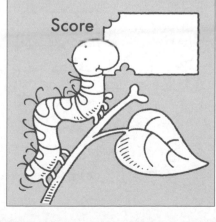

Missing numbers in subtractions up to 20

See if you can answer each set of 12 questions in one minute.

14 − ☐ = 8	16 − ☐ = 10	14 − ☐ = 3
17 − ☐ = 12	13 − ☐ = 7	17 − ☐ = 14
15 − ☐ = 5	15 − ☐ = 8	19 − ☐ = 12
18 − ☐ = 11	9 − ☐ = 3	20 − ☐ = 7
16 − ☐ = 9	20 − ☐ = 10	18 − ☐ = 9
11 − ☐ = 6	18 − ☐ = 13	12 − ☐ = 4
14 − ☐ = 7	17 − ☐ = 5	15 − ☐ = 7
10 − ☐ = 4	14 − ☐ = 6	16 − ☐ = 3
18 − ☐ = 14	15 − ☐ = 12	17 − ☐ = 9
20 − ☐ = 15	10 − ☐ = 2	11 − ☐ = 2
12 − ☐ = 4	18 − ☐ = 7	8 − ☐ = 3
17 − ☐ = 13	19 − ☐ = 7	19 − ☐ = 14

Score ☐

Score ☐

Score ☐

For answers see page 32

Mental maths mixture

See if you can answer each set of 12 questions in one minute.

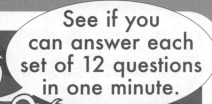

3 + 7 =	6 × 2 =	half of 5 =
11 + 4 =	18 ÷ 2 =	double 7 =
7 - 2 =	9 × 5 =	8 + ___ = 13
2 + 6 =	4 × 2 =	double 12 =
9 - 4 =	6 × 5 =	6 + ___ = 18
14 + 6 =	14 ÷ 2 =	half of 14 =
16 - 8 =	35 ÷ 5 =	double 15 =
17 + 5 =	7 × 10 =	half of 9 =
18 - 5 =	40 ÷ 10 =	14 - ___ = 7
34 - 7 =	10 × 9 =	half of 18 =
25 + 9 =	70 ÷ 10 =	double 9 =
63 - 8 =	50 ÷ 10 =	17 - ___ = 8

Score

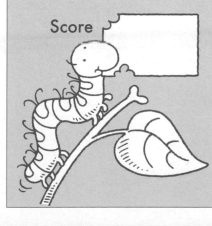

Score

Score

For answers see page 32

Page 12
The 2 times table

Column 1	Column 2	Column 3
2	8	22
4	22	14
6	16	4
8	10	24
10	18	18
12	4	8
14	12	20
16	20	2
18	14	12
20	24	16
22	2	10
24	6	6

Page 13
Dividing by 2

Column 1	Column 2	Column 3
4	3	5
7	10	1
1	4	9
3	9	6
5	7	10
9	1	12
6	5	4
12	12	7
2	8	11
11	2	3
8	6	8
10	11	2

Page 14
Multiplying and dividing by 2

Column 1	Column 2	Column 3
4	24	6
2	8	16
8	3	20
12	14	9
10	9	12
4	2	2
18	10	24
7	16	10
6	6	14
1	20	8
22	12	22
5	11	7

Page 15
The 5 times table

Column 1	Column 2	Column 3
5	20	40
10	10	10
15	35	30
20	50	55
25	25	15
30	40	35
35	5	50
40	60	20
45	45	5
50	15	45
55	30	25
60	55	60

Page 16
Dividing by 5

Column 1	Column 2	Column 3
3	5	10
2	2	7
10	6	3
7	12	8
1	3	5
12	9	2
9	10	1
5	7	11
6	1	12
8	4	4
11	11	6
4	8	9

Page 17
Multiplying and dividing by 5

Column 1	Column 2	Column 3
25	55	9
60	2	15
10	1	50
40	5	10
7	30	10
10	11	11
3	20	30
30	12	25
8	45	7
50	4	4
5	35	35
55	6	1

Page 18
The 10 times table

Column 1	Column 2	Column 3
10	70	60
20	40	40
30	20	20
40	120	100
50	60	80
60	100	30
70	10	70
80	90	10
90	30	50
100	110	120
110	50	90
120	80	110

Page 19
Dividing by 10

Column 1	Column 2	Column 3
6	5	9
9	2	11
1	8	5
3	10	1
8	6	12
10	12	3
2	7	8
12	11	2
5	1	6
7	3	4
4	9	10
11	2	7

Page 20
Multiplying and dividing by 10

Column 1	Column 2	Column 3
7	50	12
30	90	80
9	?	120
11	40	7
50	6	30
5	110	8
70	5	50
6	100	10
80	3	70
5	80	6
20	8	60
12	60	4

Doubling numbers up to 10

Column 1	Column 2	Column 3
12	16	16
16	4	18
10	18	2
6	12	4
2	8	14
18	2	8
14	16	20
20	6	6
4	10	16
8	14	10
6	20	4
14	12	12

Doubling numbers from 11 to 20

Column 1	Column 2	Column 3
32	38	32
36	24	38
24	32	26
40	26	22
22	22	30
26	34	40
38	38	34
30	28	32
22	36	28
28	22	24
34	30	36
36	40	26

Doubling numbers up to 20

Column 1	Column 2	Column 3
2	12	20
16	28	10
30	6	34
18	38	24
20	24	12
8	14	14
34	8	30
24	36	18
4	30	36
26	18	26
40	22	16
10	34	38

Halving even numbers up to 20

Column 1	Column 2	Column 3
6	9	3
4	2	9
8	6	6
7	4	8
1	7	4
10	5	7
9	1	10
3	3	2
5	7	6
4	10	1
8	2	5
2	8	9

Halving odd numbers up to 20

Column 1	Column 2	Column 3
$2\frac{1}{2}$	$7\frac{1}{2}$	$2\frac{1}{2}$
$5\frac{1}{2}$	$3\frac{1}{2}$	$6\frac{1}{2}$
$8\frac{1}{2}$	$5\frac{1}{2}$	$9\frac{1}{2}$
$1\frac{1}{2}$	$2\frac{1}{2}$	$\frac{1}{2}$
$\frac{1}{2}$	$9\frac{1}{2}$	$7\frac{1}{2}$
$9\frac{1}{2}$	$6\frac{1}{2}$	$8\frac{1}{2}$
$4\frac{1}{2}$	$4\frac{1}{2}$	$3\frac{1}{2}$
$7\frac{1}{2}$	$1\frac{1}{2}$	$5\frac{1}{2}$
$3\frac{1}{2}$	$\frac{1}{2}$	$9\frac{1}{2}$
$6\frac{1}{2}$	$8\frac{1}{2}$	$1\frac{1}{2}$
$2\frac{1}{2}$	$1\frac{1}{2}$	$4\frac{1}{2}$
$1\frac{1}{2}$	$9\frac{1}{2}$	$7\frac{1}{2}$

Halving numbers up to 20

Column 1	Column 2	Column 3
6	$5\frac{1}{2}$	$2\frac{1}{2}$
7	10	$6\frac{1}{2}$
4	2	8
$1\frac{1}{2}$	$7\frac{1}{2}$	1
10	$4\frac{1}{2}$	$9\frac{1}{2}$
$3\frac{1}{2}$	1	3
5	$8\frac{1}{2}$	7
9	$\frac{1}{2}$	9
$2\frac{1}{2}$	6	2
3	8	$8\frac{1}{2}$
8	$6\frac{1}{2}$	$4\frac{1}{2}$
$8\frac{1}{2}$	$3\frac{1}{2}$	$7\frac{1}{2}$

Missing numbers in additions up to 20

Column 1	Column 2	Column 3
6	6	9
6	8	4
10	7	6
7	9	9
6	3	4
5	11	7
5	3	7
7	2	11
6	8	6
9	4	8
5	12	12
6	3	7

Missing numbers in subtractions up to 20

Column 1	Column 2	Column 3
6	6	11
5	6	3
10	7	7
7	6	13
7	10	9
5	5	8
7	12	8
6	8	13
4	3	8
5	8	9
8	11	5
4	12	5

Mental maths mixture

Column 1	Column 2	Column 3
10	12	$2\frac{1}{2}$
15	9	14
5	45	5
8	8	24
5	30	12
20	7	7
8	7	30
22	70	$4\frac{1}{2}$
13	4	7
27	90	9
34	7	18
55	5	9

Answers